UNDER THE POMEGRANATE SUN

Melissa Hobbs

BLUE LIGHT PRESS ◆ 1ST WORLD PUBLISHING

1ST WORLD
PUBLISHING

SAN FRANCISCO ◆ FAIRFIELD ◆ DELHI

1ST WORLD LIBRARY
PO Box 2211
Fairfield, IA 52556
www.1stworldpublishing.com

BLUE LIGHT PRESS
www.bluelightpress.com
Email: bluelightpress@aol.com

BOOK & COVER DESIGN
Melanie Gendron
www.melaniegendron.com

INTERIOR ILLUSTRATIONS
David Pulsifer

COVER PHOTOGRAPHY
Melissa Hobbs

AUTHOR PHOTOGRAPH
Marianne Betterly

FIRST EDITION

Library of Congress Control Number: 2016959104

ISBN 9781421837697

Acknowledgments

Grateful acknowledgment is made to the following magazines and anthologies in which some of these poems were previously published, or accepted for publication: *Sugar Mule, Home Anthology* from Outrider Press, *Postcard Poems, Amore: Love Poems Anthology*.

My hand goes over my heart to Diane Frank for her courageous support.

A hug of thanks for my husband Tom for his unflagging wisdom.

INVOCATION

Pomegranate Juice
So ripe the red skin swells.
Fingers peal luscious flesh.
Tusked juice swirls
from tongue to toes.
Minerals enthrone the blood
and crown each heart.

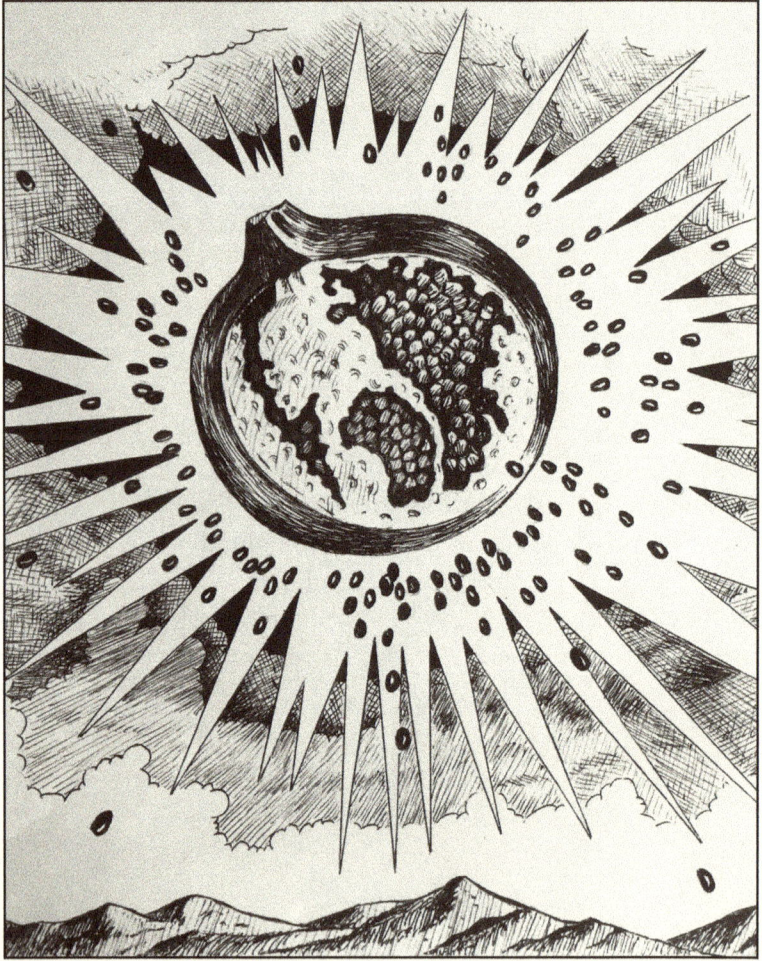

Pomegranate Sun

If the sun can crack through clouds
and shoot a bow of hope,
and the red ripening
pomegranates split pith,
then clusters of seeds must
tumble out for my hunger
and your parched lips.

In humans, the germinating
passionate impulse continues,
the amniotic sac peels away
from womb no longer needed.
Voluminous life explodes
into a familiar breath-cry, pleading
to suck, be wrapped in cloth
to breathe the burning air.

I unbelt my robe to the rainbow.
Let us dive, too.
Plummet with a parachute and roll.
Scuttle the shell cloth into a bonfire.
Make it hot enough
to lift our cries of grief
above the land of last year's smoke,
the smoke of so many old burned shells.
Between our lips the songs exhilarate
on steady wing beats.

We drink the juicy sustenance
and husk
the ash rind
of the impossible.
We flash our rubies
above the pepper smoke of misery.
We are motes that float
up the new pillars
into the pomegranate sun.

TABLE OF CONTENTS

THE PALMS IN PLEASANTON

Dawn on a Workday

Held in petals of a tulip tree
my sleeping bed floats
from helium balloon strings.

Anchored to concrete
six lanes of traffic are whipped
by the reins of a charioteer.

Trains skim along the jump rope tracks.
Souls roller coaster
the sea of city streets.

Tentacle legs wash
pools of sunlight
under the rocks of buildings,
where I grip
the shelf of a steel desk.
Abalone tongues
slide open for business.

The Palms in Pleasanton

> The palms teach us how to be tended

High on their pillars,
bobbleheads catch the trade winds.
A dozen palm trees bend
with their own umbrellas.
They have colonized the metal forest—
reams of steel, glass and backbone,
stacked window shades and sashes.

Their fronds flap orders to the power grid,
their harnessed god: *bring us electricity*
on high wires, cross states
bring us power in your claws.

Wing-clipped, we
hop from trains and cars.
Shoulder to shoulder in serried lines
through turnstiles
our red backpacks bang
as the bending hour approaches.
Our fingers bead three floors of grit.
They bet football on the fourth.

Bouncing ideas like fish between heron beaks,
they cook a memo that barbs our monitors
after we peck our passwords.

From tended cliffs we flake the gold,
gleaning remnants of the ebbing day.
Pitching our cries as clumped sandpipers,
we run with the outbound tide.

The Emulsion Angle

In the early morning,
my car lights cut through the diamond lane.
The radio racket sets me on edge.
A man has been crushed under a shipping container.
Transit workers are striking.
Two hundred thousand daily commuters
queue around the station pillars.

The guard is changing as I enter the office.
The night shift supervisor pinned
fairness, kindness and *honesty*
on the corkboard.
No blunt trauma to rank and file.
No answers will fill empty bellies and hearts.

Tweets gallop in like Robin Hood
on my cell phone as if they could strike.
Not like my mother the sheriff,
who wouldn't commit her mouth
to an opinion, only a frown.
That's over.

They are mobbed against
the hurricane fence of intelligence,
abuse of work, the unanswered promise,
the absence of soap and towels.
Head tipped in the mirror, practice the speech.
Manage the appropriate deep eye sympathy.

I am merely plugged in on a higher peg
which requires an emulsion of response.
Don't get dragged under tears and metal.
Cream rises.
Float with a smile.

Passageway into June

My bike rolls the Ohlone Greenway.
Wilding plants elbow me,
shooting the routine commute,
arriving at the station bike cages.
Faces on the train tick
over the pillars, concrete is not all
that propels the June merger of races.

Rocked by frequent trains:
elderberry canes jazz,
redbud leaves rumba,
mustard flowers fandango
with half-a-millennia of newcomers.
Anise, oat grass, dandelion
sprouted first from under the hooves
of Arabian horses, the boot spurs
of conquistadores.
Under the human hammering
for metal in California,
native and immigrant plants
released via wind, sun bending,
and by rain grew side by side.

My handlebars tap
the amphora of green ore
pouring from a solstice
not bound by commute clocks.

Braising the Boss

So you didn't sleep well last night,
what do I care?
So you heaved through years of loyalty,
a wife scraping for your boss,
only now he's jilted you for retirement.
So you held your arm in civil service salute
and he never saluted back.
Do you expect me to cock my ear to your opera
about dragging his tie
down to small claims court?
So what if he invited a small swarm
to a private luncheon,
slamming the door in your face?

He was the one who never said thank you
when you gathered the cats to yowl.
Didn't he abscond with your balloons,
paint his name on their stars,
then release the helium,
boasting like a horse's ass
through the cracked door of his office?
After all, his effigy was included
in our 3D clone collection of managers.
Were you holding your breath
for a gold engraved invitation
to his rickety fire escape,
carried in a diaper by a stork?

Peach Pits

To make a laptop from peaches,
slice half wise, spoon out pits,
sun-dry and stack three per inch.
Slide in the motherboard.
Stick alligator clips on diagonal corners
and plug into a skuzzy serial port.
Watch the fuzz fly.

To change a waste paper basket
into a parking garage,
cut a hole in the side with wire cutters.
Shrink yourself and your car
with the downloadable app to ant size.
You can drive inside
before the downpour of peach pits
shoots from the board of trustee's tower.
This will protect you
until a peach pie bomb
flies through your cubicle.

Chihuahua News Service

His backbiting criticisms fizz
humidity across the office horizon.
Summer rumors rumble.
The drained water cooler
welcomes a downpour
of discussion about his probation.

I pat his head to calm his hide,
but point out his scratch work,
and he huddles under the table
slobbering, and dribbles the carpet.

The Chihuahua News barks
at the boss's paperweight.
It will be thrown at his camel nose
and jack-ball tongue.

Takeover in the Board Room

While our hearts and minds sew
words onto their overcoats,
the wearers don't stop
bruising the airplane aisles.

They offer muddy promises between flights,
when the home office fountain flows green.
They hold out shine to stick on
our straight time paychecks.

Let us brush their robes
with rounded shadows, our reminders,
and blow off the crescent gloom
of their own eclipse of sunlight.

We don't watch free movies of repeated journeys.
We'll underline the subtitles with silk thread.
We'll wear Stone Age shoes to clomp the lies
when the board reunion door opens.

Their buttonholes open when tying shoes.
Let us slip off their furry overcoats
and cast the silk into a rope bridge,
where castoffs catapult
into the dark matter of black holes.

Metamorphosis

Bagged trash
bulges by the neon elevator.
I whine and whistle to coworkers.
Who doesn't ache for the marine life,
diving to the bottom portal
of this ship of a building?
Our shoes slip off the gangplank.
Jetsam castoffs trail us
from the tragedy of work.
Under the puddled sidewalks,
aquamarine ripples from the street light.

At the train escalator, I kick
my disguise of work legs
into the recycle bin.
By the time we reach the platform,
only a few eyebrows rise
when my red hair sprouts long over my tail fin.
Mermaids here usually meet glacial stares.

Capture the Sun

As I threw my camisole out the train window,
the sun was fizzing ginger to a small guitar.
Rosebud mothers whined, *you're not supposed*
to go topless; they'll go blind watching.
As I jived from high heels and trotted out hiking boots,
the oaken conductor ordered, *don't*
touch the third rail, or you'll die trying.
As I dropped pant suit and shimmied into twill slacks,
keystone cops moaned, *don't pedal your bike*
across three lanes of traffic, unless your tongue likes rubber.

Last night, when I should be sleeping,
I cowed fretful under a closet of voices
and their chin-tied legends.
Before midnight, I snatched my ID
and leapt through the furnace of the rude,
not blind, naked, electrocuted,
or flattened by tire tracks in a cartoon strip.

Their anvil words are melting with the old sun.
My rose is blooming, open to all insects.
My trees ground the lightning bolts without scars.
My cops shoot only recycled rubber bullets.

There's an orb just above my belly.
It sparks with consonants and branches
between my handlebars.
This diva is welcoming the wise women
from the East and West to weave an orb web
between earth and heaven
and whatever lies in-between.

Ransom behind the Drapes

Office workers don't show their tuxedos.

Our fingers blister
fretted keyboards,
while cello strings glide
over concert quaffed heads.
For eight hours our turtle-necks
poke a flat screen.
Huskies moan in the window,
You won't ever come home.

Our fingers are wagering keystrokes,
while race horses chomp alfalfa.
We mouse for hours
through mixed data fields.
Starved for sunlight,
our children's faces flatten in the glass.

Our fingers are trapped in elevators,
while stage mime hands
raise the roof.
For hours moles tunnel
in the freeway dark.
Balancing water glasses,
our husbands hold back the drapes.

Colors of Commerce

Commuters leap from doors, stampede escalators,
and escape the competition of hooves
down the staircase chute.
Their nostrils flare for home.
Stale coffee, pork bellies and bank notes
slide under some woman's antiseptic spray,
while charcoal clouds the sun.

Pacing into the turnstile, I'm a frame
around which their tinctures flow.
I think of Tintoretto.
Their forearms billow with light.
The umber walls linger behind
orange hard hats, chartreuse vests,
pink, blue and purple dyed hair.
Below their haloed faces,
the color of commerce is black.

While Venetian sailors rowed
lime white boats in indigo to dock,
these commuters hoard space with gray
laptops strapped against their chests.

I offer mint to freshen old oils,
but no whites of eyes take in my palette.
Ear buds fill their pointed ears.
Azure LEDs enter their psyches.
This treasure cask of cochineal
is buried too close to their lives.

Their eyes will trample into sunset.
Each black pupil is a chandelier
looking for illumination.

VALLEJO

Vallejo's Bankruptcy

Nectar is scanty at the crest
of the Bay Area Ridge Trail
this year with no rain.
Only Sherpa plants
are green this late,
anise, thistle, mustard
covered by bumble bees.

In the land bowl below
amid thousands of houses,
the city buys lunch
for half its children.

I haven't turned to salt
staring at crackling grasses.
Not turning away from seeds
or children—some will flourish.

As the city sheds another skin,
wind is the viper of old promises.
It whips a split tongue,
when eyes turn opaque to agreements
crumpling last year's union rules.
Hissing debates.
Retirements liquidate.

Police and firefighter faces
are emptied holes
on the billboard downtown.

Salt drips off my forehead.
Something pushes the blindness
of somersaulting from the ridge top
over those swaggering in alleys.
Some are bumblebees harvesting what's left.
Some snakes are healing our eyes.

Guarding Washington Park

Soccer players kick vigilance
on the green at Washington Park.
Brazen bronzed arms link
a fortress around the neighborhood.

Joshua's army drives dented cars,
cruising the corners.
They hunger for grazing pastures-
children beginning to throb.
Fresh from the safe deposit box,
Joshua's gold tooth anoints his face,
while his wolves spray graffiti
on walls of the grocery.

His lures dangle promises.
He blows mosaics of smoke
from ziplock bags.
Children's eyes and legs wobble,
naive of his jangled mornings.
Too late they might discover
their sprouted acorn hands are trapped.
They might as easily be seeds
devoured between the wolves' teeth.

On the soccer field, strong legs
kick the bass back to the alleys,
bump da bump, thump ra rump.
Children wheel, laugh
and trample the mowed grass.
Their tongues pulsate
English, Spanish, Tagalog
across Vallejo.

Volcanic Bungalow

The deadbolt unsnaps.
The key opens my marigold door.
Inside my volcano collapses.
The neighbor's son, God-fearing
splayed the legs of an old purse
over the bedroom floor.
He knocked out money and ransacked
jewelry from my drawers.
He exposed his brazen escape
by replacing the kitchen curtain
raw insides out.

At the back door, no fingers or ghosts
have tampered or kneed the door lock,
but Wall Street drives the alley behind
the bungalows of El Dorado Street.

What fizzes in the basement?
It's the sound banks make
stealing dreams from our safes.
My roof is caving into the basement,
as if a ton of fallen oak leaves
from some unseen dump truck
buried my home in flammable waste.

An unseen someone knew the pilot light
would ignite and set fire to the leaves
in a pretense to kill termites,
who fly away in the sparks.
I hear "that's just business,"
and, " I'm a business man."
My spanking new stainless
stove, fridge and washing machine
sink into the real estate lava.

Yellow Bamboo

A homeless mass dumps what remains
from last night's beer bust next door
into his black garbage bag.
He recycles.
He sallies through the unlatched double gate.
He waters the yard between his barrel chested hands.
A squirrel jockeys and chatters
from the concave roof of a car garage.

My screen door stands ajar
and screeches on its hinge.
After I moved into the neighborhood,
Joe's arm healed into mangles.
My rear window sights his driveway.
Blood paints our curbs.
The earthquake cracks in my house ache.
A neighbor's email smacks shame: click delete.
From the castle moat neighbor,
We all know the color of crime.

After I plant it, yellow bamboo grows two feet
from my fence stakes into that bare dirt yard.
Their youngest girl faces my fence alone,
cries for hours, breaking two hearts.

Redeeming Persephone

1. Persephone was kidnapped by Hades
    before her flower buds bloomed.
    She couldn't return until she ate
    the hard pitted pomegranate—
    elixir of winter seasons.

2. In Vallejo, some families were sucked
    into the winter of bankruptcy.
    The gang of Bank Gods feasted
    on real estate flooding underground.

3. Winter hatched out mosquitoes,
    droning the sleepers
    on one sheet-free mattress.

4. While parents drove all night for work,
    children imprinted on finger smooth screens.
    Grandparents' folk music drowned
    by helicopter, car alarms and jake breaks.
    Throats were buried
    deep as native creeks by freeways.
    The promise to win was synthesized
    in a handheld mirror of myth.
    The children pricked their fingers
    to test if they were human.

5. If bent-over backs of Hell-baked hope
    could bulldoze cruelty from the creeks,
    then crickets and frogs would leap
    and wildflowers would sprout.

6. Some family hearths hadn't been
   kidnapped under a winter of debt.
   Kindled by Vulcan's crackling logs,
   and warmed brick promises, they built
   breastplates of strength, drank tusked juice
   of Persephone's harvest.
   The red blood of bone marrow
   tumbled out for their community.
   They held onto their hand woven rope
   over the whirlpool of demons.

7. Husbands and wives slogged all ways
   to bake bricks in sunlight
   that myths alone couldn't finish.

Lace Lattice

I can make a mile safe, I cajole myself,
amid the men wobbling in crosswalks
who can't remember home.
From the car repair to my home
there's no silver bubble.
Abandoned railroad tracks accept
tires and mattresses.
Adult bookstore videotapes are stripped
to sell half price.
White Slough furniture stores clamber
from pine forests, as if equal to hardwoods.
Georgia Street car lots beg
with reclaimed luxury cars.
We want to go home with you!
The new lawn ornament is ketchup.

Skidding around sidewalk trash,
my craving begins for an orderly city.
As fountains need hardware,
the animal brain needs the frontal cortex.
Our corpus callosums should be latticed
as fences between neighbors.
To lattice our nerves with calm words,
"Good fences make good neighbors."
I crawl under a fence to reach a stranger's door,
evading gunfire.

Joe ID'd the man who stole his daughter's car
and the neighborhood.
Freed on bail, revenge returned.
It's the wrong time of year to fertilize
his roses with arm and lung blood.
Nuts fall, cars backfire, adrenalin jumps.

The base reverberates our lattices.
"Tend your own garden, water your bamboo,"
chatters the squirrel, who bites the apple.
Neighborhood gardens sprout rats and bullet holes.
I peek through bamboo waiting
to shadow a solid fence line,
to stumble, and return to my car.
I'll water my bamboo,
let it spread by underground runners.

Crashing in Town

I gave you ten years and you returned
from the Peace Corps unsoftened.
Lesotho hardship, decay, it cut you
you say, as your airplane leaks
spit as if it were rain.
You became landlocked, too
and never made pilgrimage
beyond the country to the deep ocean.
Earth humbles to gather your shell casings.
You vaunt over the HIV tombs.
Your lips take ten minutes to compass
the *hours* you drove to find us
from the airport to Vallejo.
The broken wings of someone
who forgot how to fly.

White's Slough

Hot thighs blister
in sunburned tidal shifts.
The briny sheen
stinks like menopause.
Used fertility isn't nice.

We want to hear bulldozers
smother that muck.
Pave it into obedience.
Turn that mess into money,
the city chamber choruses.

Every summer day
waterfowl soloists
congratulate their grandmas.
In the orchestra
web feet untruss
insects and crustaceans.
Their beaks fill.
Baby craws grow.

Birds clatter, so frivolous.
An earthquake jellies
the ground so seldom,
we'll never need a buffer
for a red moon tide
a rising ocean,
or a toxic bloom.

Earth Conditions

The world is a glorious place to die in,
if you don't mind the rainbow lacking a few shades.
When everything is fine in heaven,
even they must listen to our work songs.

The world is a glorious place to die in,
if you don't mind seeing souls flying up with torn wings.
Or maybe children rising from rib bare starvation,
sometimes carrying what colors small arms can gather.

This world is a glorious place to die in
if you don't mind the orations of minds
whose words pool on pavement.
Maybe errant priests kneeling naked,
or station hugging firemen pleading for a pension,
when at last the gravity barbs release
from the bankrupt city.

Yes, this world is the most splendid place to pass through
if you don't mind the hot oil smell of a working elevator
trying to rise to the 13th floor in a four floor building.

SONGS FROM HEART MOUNTAIN

Eating at Nations

At San Pablo and Central
neon and fluorescent
dance all night
around the breakfast special,
before the dawn-to-dusk fast.

Arab spring on the flat screen.
The glare-faced general tallies
eyes of red-rimmed widows
walking into the desert
girding up their loins,
rough leather against burning sand.

It's about intent.
Build a temple in a place
where others give up.

I order fish and munch
catsup with fries on formica.
This place serves gratefulness.

Mirrored plate glass dawns
to phone poles in the parking lot.
A world of homeless hair
weaves its combed headdress.

The Gleaming Prison

I step over the moat
to Akka's prison in Israel.
Brighter than sunlight
reeds release the ancient songs
from the window
from the dry bed
they give wings to the walls.

The white handkerchief waved
from that upper window
unfurling to pilgrim eyes
a banner to snap,
perfume to wipe their tears.

I climb each day to the gate,
rippling the chants
and the moat fills with salt water.
This bridge of earth
is a prison
brighter than sunlight.

Fasting on Heart Mountain

While the world at sea level shoves along,
during the fast, kites tales snap,
up on heart mountain
with audible mantras.
I must scale the massive shoulders
to pull down the strings.
They hold truth—
mother light rising from fire-
assigned to everyone.
Free flying, the kites taunt me,
hovering at the ridge top.

The first three days I get close enough
to feel the undulating current,
as if I could grasp the tips.
My back stings with sweat.
Thirst thwarts my throat into silence.
Begging for the end of each fasting day,
my anger fire extinguishes.
A rock alcove trickles
into the makeshift camp.
I chant prayers and the wind
sighs between cracks.

As midnight blue evolves to mauve,
trials of the prior day melt away.
If spirit masters my feet,
I will mount the mirage.
What dry joints I have shrink into swords
and I fence with razorback pillars.
Their sparks spur heels over loose rocks.
Judgments shrivel,
but my face won't unwrinkle.

Sixteen days of pilgrim dust ruddies my face.
I cling to the sweat of the unknown brave
who came before. Together with essence
I'm closer than ever to the kite tails.
Maybe their peregrine arms
pulled in opposing directions.
Down in the hazy valley love shunts,
waking, sleeping, dying.
Faith pulls upward
to kites, free of strings.

I'm waving from a cliff,
but the gauzy world sinks
into the jostling sea.

Together as wings my arms sweep
bone heavy, raisin sweet.
The final three days will witness less sleeping,
more jumping to catch the kite tails
rolling off the top of this world.

Behind the Evening News

1. Public Persona

Khan scours grief off
cakes on innocence,
teddy bear eyes, baritone lips
he has five seconds.
Chin lifted, red lights flash on,
cameras roll in, he
buoys up America
on flat screen TVs.

Behind his clown face,
remote from fatherland
and his father's hands,
his wife holds their daughter's fingers.
Intensive care tubes suck her air.
A sea of drowning shrapnel. . .

Flash: Kandahar, Baghdad, Aleppo.
Lines of car skeletons, white sheets,
a mob of necks stretch, pump arms.
No rights drive down these streets.
Khan's eyes reach every throat.
His face *is* family at six.

They will never see or know
which bomb or country.
So long as camera light is radiant,
she will breathe. Spiders fret across the lens.
Too soon the valentine blinks black,
machines give up their whine.
Khan's shoulders punch forward.
He scarified his time in sacrifice.

Prayers for the Passing

Chairs gather around a fireplace.
Families leave their shoes at the door.
Hands hold prayer books,
holding breath, waiting.
The host parades shoes on a tray.
His molasses voice peddles.
If you help, God willing,
showers of answers will flood your prayers.
I have to sell fifty pair to pay my mortgage,
or you make a donation!
Khan slides his shoes onto a crowded shelf,
surrenders his knees to the floor.
He becomes *Khanitra*, a tool of his people.
He feels for wallet, stretched fabric empty.
A mulla barricades the door of search.
Right shoes huddle like chaste wives.
The left have gone missing.
Someone whispers *look in the basement.*

Hidden where tarantulas crawl,
dozens of left shoes pay a bride price.
Nothing left after shoes.
Behind the home walls
their chants are water spraying off a cliff.
Every voice gathers in the alcove.
Khanitra calls across the chasm.
Our shoes are hidden, our money taken,
homelands burned, children dead.
Yet, in prayer we are floating up,
closer to the moon.

Every Halo

Blue fills the room.
Potential halos every face.
I find the universe here,
filled with points of light,
filled with words.

After three days the newspaper attacks.
My feathers bathe in gutter water.
Is street oil supposed to slick the lice itch?
The news is a pawn broker of camellias.
Beneath my hijab
ripe loquats dehydrate.
What can quell this?

But, see the charred barbecue grill,
dull lawnmower blades,
rusted hedge clippers.
You're the rusted blades
that burn my meat, woman.

Blue hides in goose down.
I'm facing my own pilgrimage.
I find comfort in antibiotic words.
I expunge bleached blood.
Inner eye turns toward memory
knowing every phrase
has a bird peck of light.
At probate the great will
offers blue to every halo.

Wages in War Zones

Quick, I only have
a few breaths left.
Find my wife,
kiss my brothers.
Hold my children for me, won't you?

You have no whispers left
to make amends.
But we will carry on the war
against your trivial belief.
Fire power ricochets
around brick corners.
Yours is one of many bodies
whose clothing we shred.
Drink your last pilgrimage.

Mosaics of clothes go cold.
Pomegranates spatter.
The naked fill the street.

Women spread rugs on sand
outside of the burning town.
They hope by night
to sneak back for water
collecting what's left
for the hollow children.

A Cup or an Urn

At the beach where snow cones were invented
a hand held camera shakes history.
Neptune Beach has vanished.
Sandpipers run and cluster about.
Where are their grandparents
clean picked bones?

At a stray gull call, they fly up.
The scarf splits into white and brown.
Over deeper water they circle
return together
in the shallowing outbound bay
and come down upon crustaceans,
pecking for their lives.

A man with a cup or an urn
wanders around the edge.
He holds white ashes, or sweet grief.

He bends without breaking
letting the ash spill and return
a mound of memory gathering
as it washes seaward.

Hearing My Own Words

Awakening me from sleep,
the starchy squeak of my angry talk.
Into a room of friendly ears
I dropped a sack of flour last night.
Tomorrow their tongues slide
my raw dough over kitchen tables.
My name will linger, an aftertaste
that will muffle hearing
with thickened ignorance.

They open a staircase door
and throw what they know of me
into a basement labyrinth,
where abasement floods out
again and again in winter rains.

I've watched slick remarks
fresco the office walls, read the news
at two a.m., another suicide
from cyberbullying.

I unwind the night window.
Clerestory hands test the soft wind.
The cooing of pigeons cools
the dovecot of my brick head.

When the house finch chatters morning,
I will tear open the bitter rind
and drink up the cleansing juices
ripening in the hidden orchard.

Sable Angel

Unmistakable as age
spots on my arms,
was I not supposed to see you
hovering forward of my bed
at midnight?

Am I not supposed to resist
your stroke of fate,
waiting to stop morning,
different from the life giving
angels of other hours?

For what purpose should I arm
white blood cells, if not for life?
What good the antibodies against
the splinter that throbs my finger,
when with you it is death
to what I know on earth.

Across my sleeves at night
your bristles hover without haste,
waiting to suck my last breath
and fill me with reckoning.

Paradise Garden

The sea breeze lifts the foliage
from tree trunks with a whisper
so pure, the leaves cast salt
from their wounds.

Having cast salt
into the open-armed air,
their lance-like shapes shake
free from iron chains as well.

Unspoken memories are salt.
The chains chafed their necks.
When surrendered to the sea
They disintegrate the manmade
dam between land and sea.

Tongues that could not speak,
chant with life-giving whispers.
Their voices breach to the sea.

Xylem Tea

For Rebecca, Susan, Connie and the others

After the cup comes up
and heat pours down my throat;
After sap climbs spine stairs,
and buzzes my heart;
After one more day
smolders prison walls
into ash and cinders;
I will build xylem atriums
for echoing praise in sinew songs.
Flower petals trail
from my garden
to dazed coworkers.

Winter Opulence

The naked upward thrust
of icy boughs
outstretches to the clouds.
The proof of life—
rib buds swell
under the amnion
of the blue canopy.

In winter,
I remember
the migrating hermit thrush
with angelic song,
under the brush of sorrow.
That summons raises a call
to the lazuli awning,
hoping for more than echo.

Unwrap my eyes to sunlight
unfolding from winter solstice.
I offer my breath
clouds of wealth
to breed little fires
of leaf splendor
from these skeletons.

TREKKING THROUGH FAMILY

Ode To Women in Father's Family Tree

By calling each of your names,
I invoke you from weed covered,
lichen worn marble.

Staunchly upright, your stone faces
defeat death in century old photos.
But, you doubt if my candle
can illumine the calico of your clothing,
sewn between my fingers.
Doubt frays your shirtwaist cuffs
where you squared yourselves
to your husbands, stern or strong.

Turned over from your graves,
you say Tuesday with my father's drawl.
He dug in his heels, a scientist,
a sturdy-legged wanderer dissecting
smartweeds under a thimble lens.
Publishing research, he splashed
between pond stones.

Back behind the barnyard
some Cronus of a father
turned Dad over a stump
and smacked at deviation,
until cornfields and weed seeds
became Dad's quietest rooms.

Grandfather's sullen sepia glare
defined manhood with medicine,
a Model A, and a carriage barn.
Gertrude, you huddled in a black coat
over your embarrassed belly,
with husband proud to his family,
and Dad forthcoming.

Before Indiana, the generations
misty-eyed, male-voiced,
they summed you up as the unknown sisters.
I spade up your first names in the census.
How did you weave linen and sew clothing?
Did you endure the tumpline of bushel baskets?
Did you horde the handful of fabric scraps
and sew them for your own shrouds?

The last woman's burial unearthed
an old quilt from a chest of pine.
Touch great grandmother's stitches
sewn by kerosene light.
Yet, her arm pulls squares and diamonds
over my shoulder to cover
the nights where I disappear.

Dad's herbarium hinges
would close over my mouth.
You all here, please hover behind me
and blow open my voice, born of cloth
stronger than a cold frame of weeds.

Fingers on the Strings of Family

My oldest brother's banjo
pushes wind through wild onion grass
as fast as I can weed it.
His songs, adoring the first born male,
where droning women and girls rake fruit,
are the trimmings of my heredity.
His bluegrass mustache dangles over my backyard.
My dirty fingernails and rank hands
have trimmed my labyrinth of onion domination.
Bare shoulders, naked as humus,
are exposed to the icy heat of spring.
I capture my own verses.
My lungs call over the backyards to the gene horde
release your shadowing wings.

My autoharp sings to the neighborhood birds.
My children sprout like pin feathers.
Their naked skins throb to fill and fledge.
Whosh, their wings turn alien
and their scent ghastly, as they complain
of onion on my breath. They bully my thyme,
argue with my rhubarb, smother my penstamon.
They drown out autoharp arpeggios
and galloping banjo horses.
Their drumming wings press my elbows
not as I, weeding to clear the land,
but rolling to bury the family of onion tradition,
once and for all with friendly rocks:
sequoia gold, chocolate flagstone,
three rivers tumble.
Avalanches cascade from their wing beats.

Family Reunion in Taiwan

Crossing Sun Moon Lake
in a one cylinder
put-put boat,
three generations floated with Monet.
Remember the straw hats
over slacks,
and ivory ancestors
carved on chopsticks?
I do whenever
I Ching throws
the joyous lake.

Dad's Leaves

Some trees drop their leaves
in gusts, or in slow motion.
October winds
leave everything naked,
except for evergreens.

You flushed to scarlet,
then blanched
left the bed.
You departed without air.
The oxygen tank kept flowing.

Naked like any old man.
Limbs going slack under the sheet.
Gurney rolled out the front door
by black-suited tight-lipped orderlies,
left me to a fall of fire danger,
scarlet eyes and white handkerchiefs.
Wringing out of a deep forest
are the Latin named botanicals
you loved, your last breath
an encyclopedia of leaves.

The Self-Same Bird

The red-eyed vireo
sang his sweet song
to the green grass
of grandma's backyard,
as now toward the farm porch swing
the self-same song sings.
We read the Wednesday
obituary in stiff
Sunday clothes that itch.

Is it the same song
as long years ago,
when the air between notes
from tomato factories
scented our play,
and now echoes where
corn and soybean trucks roar
down the horizon road?

It's not the same bird.
We can't find where
he was laid to rest.
The newspaper print renders
grandma in black and white.
Her muscular song and ears
heard some other bird
sing those same songs
we now hear.

Seckel Pear Hootenanny

Swept from under the Seckel pear tree
by the brother who reaches
to the top of the rake,
the pile of unwanted fruit
in my five-year-old hands
becomes the walls of homes,
streets of a village,
and the families themselves.

The party begins on pebbled asphalt,
on a cul-de-sac in Ohio.
One by one, each pear soul
is sung to life from the heap.
In my rag apron,
I carry them over the road edge.
At first initiation, they resist tearing.
My nubby fingers shove pear skin
in sacrifice across the sharp tarry stones.
Their remnant flesh ages to burnt sienna.
I run to the pile to retrieve new workers.
All must walk or drive to school or work.

When their roundness flattens,
they become grandparents, unable to offer
more than memory to the clan.
The old ones wait in juice spots
for the Saturday night barn dance.
As I thrust the pear families
in under the eaves, the old ones cheer.
My hootenanny chorus rises
overhead, circling to the apple,
mulberry and pawpaw trees
that feed the neighborhood.

Once an hour, a pick-up truck
barrels over Beal Drive.
As I retreat to the pear trunk,
the driver smiles and waves.
His tires crush happenstance victims.
Hovering on the edge of life,
their stem ends tremble.
Soon the pear children accompany the pear hearse
to the milkweed and Queen Ann's lace graveyard.
The towering elm sways with dust.

The next morning I watch
our calico cat hit by a car,
on the far side of the state route.
Father grimaces and shovels her up.
I can't pet her head or hear her purr,
buried under the Seckel Pear Tree.

Peppermint for Clowns

Having transplanted
the five gallon pot into the yard,
she comes to love the peppermint
more than her husband.

Sweat sore, hips kneeling
to weed turgid wild onion,
flooding downhill from in-laws,
she aches to savor tea oil.

Close by the patch
the towhees nest in the plum.
If she returns the second spring
they will nest and fledge yearly.

Husband's mower blades hack
to split the green grass.
She wands a magic wall
with arms, like a bank guard.

If he returns from the mower shed
scrubbed free of gossip,
maybe she can brew for him
a pot of peppermint tea.
Maybe she can laugh at the stain
that slips off his slacks,
and she slips off her clown red gloves.

Sonoma Fall Return

I slog through thigh deep weeds
where years ago, the fog of motherhood
composted my skin, giving it for children
under the living redwood trees
of my Eden.
Returning to my nest land,
I had forgotten the jabbing path.
Remnants of green gorse I tried to burn
attack through clothing, even now dead,
as the dark trees grow a forest.

On a limb above my head
sparrow lures a wish tail of blackberry leaves,
and mottled bruise-dried fruit.
Chicadees scat old uncertainties
to the snap of my hip joints.
They scold with prongs
from nests of their future.

The dog run to the stream
is overgrown by poison oak.
She barked under the cloud high fir
that now stands over the home
of the other bone-dried crone.

They were my trees, too.
Their rawness healed,
closed the doorway to my wild.
The dangling moss drips father
and mother into the ravine.
The stream runs year round,
but it isn't anyone's to keep.

Vestige of Marriage

A copy of an 1815 gingerbread recipe,
and Dad's mincemeat clings
on a sheet of red paper,
almost obliterated by vinegar spots.
Whoever threw the cursive words,
dropped projectiles into slave quarters.
This sheet, wrapped around 3 by 5 cards,
was stowed between hardbound cookbooks.
Each year of the last dozen
one egg escaped the oven,
but when hatched,
never grew feathers.

Stolen Oranges

I knew the raccoon was in the backyard
when the first ripe oranges disappeared,
five years after our dream was planted.
As I trekked compost through mud to the bin,
a hollow emptiness inhabited the bottom
tree branch in Christmas Eve rain.

In the tunnel that darkens memory,
I lugged the dwarf tree
from the nursery to my car.
I twisted on a red bow, wrote on the gift tag:
To be planted in compost and watered,
as a banner of your promise.

In the meantime, you filled concrete plans
with a meter long pour, round earthquake ties,
bolted to the hip of a remodeled foundation.
You and I consummated the folk tale
with paint, brushing our colors on walls.

The masked beggar was not hindered
by snores from our heated house.
It ripped down oranges,
rolled them under the vines,
and split them four ways to Sunday.

Winter rain is fueling the flaming green leaves.
Even if an earthquake takes the house
and more oranges are stolen,
we have eaten the better fruit.

Tahoe Granite

At Tahoe's Big Meadow
a blue grouse
drums
deep
in the conifers.

We eat green melon
on flat granite
after a hike.
The sun tugs shadows away,
beating heat into
June's longest day.

Today's trek floats
meadow wings—
monarch, viceroy, copper
above our hardy leather boots.
Buddha climbs ten thousand steps.

We nudge
conglomerate
boulders at Round Lake,
breathless with lapping blue,
bow to birds
our bragging cousins,
flicker, chickadee, pewee.

Toe our shoe marks in sand,
pollen-filled footprints
already girdle gaunt trees.

On the far shore
quartz dikes split
ancient basalt.

We watch birds
peck sand shards
and blue green pollen
for their alpine lives.

Between my woman's ribs
a rift rises to give you
one of my stardust wings.

My Corolla Sister

You let me stroke your forest green
so that I didn't have to grieve.

Secure behind your steering wheel
we crested Jonive Hill and forded Salmon Creek
five days a week to work.
Naked to the county wags,
I drove blindly, before the sawmill sawdust burner
blew ice cream cone relatives
across the road, shattering my house walls.

After an argument with an in-law,
who claimed to be a relative,
I backed you into the barbecue
abandoned in the driveway,
painted your scars with fern paint.
I meditated in your driver's seat
and you hummed.
This was before my kangaroo mouse
threw his paws away.

When your sister Tercel was hit
head-on by a drunk driver,
my daughter survived.
You steamed up tea for the wake.
The hulk haunted your parking space
for weeks, waiting for insurance
to make the proper burial.

My ghost floated over work tire rhythms,
through Halloween and All Souls Day,
when the rains washed away
the sawdust remnants of my home.

I picked a white rose
for your rearview mirror.
As it dried, you drove me to give
sacred stanzas to a stranger,
but his windshield wipers
flossed away my ink.

My dog's hair embraced your seat when we moved.
Even when I spilled bean stew
meant for a potluck on your carpet,
you never faltered, or misfired
anger through the foot pedals.

Through culverts of adolescence
you guided my daughter.
With breastplates you carried her tribe.
Dearer than the blood of in-laws,
you carried me through life rooms,
humming a tune my grandmother knew.

Bouquet

Our wedding photo quavers
diagonal bands of sky
on the ship of the dresser.
Turquoise curtains sail
away from cold glass.

We are smiling
from our bowsprit
of spiraling sunflowers.

STERNUM WORDS

Sternum Words

for Tom C.

I sit at your feet listening.
A torch of earth-core liquefies
and low pitches spray
from your mouth.
You, the tight-throated volcano
pump mineral ash to sprinkle
my glacial snow pages.

I stretch to catch
what doesn't freeze
or burn my hands.
My baby volcano smolders.

With sternum words,
you set me on fire.
I nod, not knowing how
to use your power to powder
my charcoal for words.

I have your fire stones
cooking in my basket
of ground grain.
Do I stir you
with mother's walnut spoon
or silver tongs?

Aria

After your voice levitates the ceiling,
the full house rises
from the hardwood echo chamber
where you honed your sounding board.
After the floating smiles
remove their teeth from your heart
and stretch their bedrock ribs with a sigh,
happiness spills into a reserved seat.
Laugh when your listeners,
who once used purses to skirmish,
fatten the arm rests
and tip their ears from the balcony.
Laugh when faces resembling yours
catch a glimpse of sky.

Curing Olives

Because she was a novice,
the olive curer
mixed salt and water unevenly
in the gallon jars,
leaching tannin in sapling days.
Some fruit plunked down,
bitter and salty, in her third season.

She walks in the desert of the olive press.
A poem floats over the oasis.
Her brother sees mirage
and won't touch the oil.
His sun rises from crinkled vellum—
a volume whose capital letters
carve truth in barbed wire.

She inhales her cigarette of creed,
blows it over the veins of bay and bamboo
that cloister the patio.
In curing come
drops of sweet oil.

A Squirt of Lemon

It's good to squirt lemon on a poet
just as you would on a fish dinner.
Tartness puckers meat from gills.
Seagulls cry, pitching
beach-strewn fragments.
The poet gathers them in her bucket.

Twenty-nine years after womb prayer,
the poet's son shoulders no ease.
He hoisted a fisherman's tackle
above the sinking boat of that high tide.
The fishwife cinched albatross laws
around his Samaritan neck.
His hands were cuffed behind his back,
and full beard faced black-robed justice.
The poet heard Jonah ranting
during her son's three days
in the underground jail.

It's good to accept those times
when no words become the catch of the day.
The boat scuppers scratch her scales.
She washes overboard
and drags the watery wake
catapults into the eddy.

When earth's rain sprinkles
the toothy leaves of lemon balm,
it's good to drink that tea
a ladder up her spine.
A tick hatches
crawls up the pant leg
of the meditating poet.

Like a pricked finger on a spinning wheel,
followed by the red bite kiss
from the miniature prince,
a new poem hatches
with a squirt of blood.

Elephant Mother's Day

If only mother elephant wrapped her trunk
farther around him,
and threw her swinging bridge against the lions,
maybe he would have mimicked
the gray guard and sniffed ahead for the scent.

As it is, she comes upon him alone.
Hind legs out quivering, skin ripped,
bellowing, bleeding from spoil.

At the thunder of her legs,
the pride hightails
into carnivorous grass.
They lounge, abundance
of time in their weight.

The other elephant mothers guard
the wallow, dry of water.
So many months without rain,
his cracked rib heaves.
She stands, a stench to mark her perimeter.

On the morrow, sun-bake heats her back.
He's gone from the curl of her trunk.
She throws up dust to cover his scent.
She trails him half a day.
So fast he was born, grew and is gone.

A Rippling Inch of Hope

Gray-green February sulks
below the rim line of Wildcat Canyon.
Six weeks catching sunlight,
willow wands summon pollen.
Dryness tears new leaves.
They yearn—rain.

My stout khaki legs seeking
kinship walk all day.
Cold depresses insects in holes.
Fish scale clouds promise,
but dam up the rain.

What agitates branches?
The tiniest olive-gray bird looms.
Orange streaks his crown,
and circus tent stripes
whiten his cheeks.
His voice is a pillar of service.
His baffling jumps
summit the leaf-feathered trees
and give every female
a banner song for her ova.

I fix my gaze through the gauze of trees.
May all drab days be fleeting,
and your stripe become a winged ladder.
Let me glide with your flight,
the meteor of a greater promise.
Let the rains come on time.

St. Paul's at 43rd and Judah

A tall steeple and simple walls.
Like plainsong, the paint—
closely crafted mauve, ivory, eggshell,—
doesn't stand out,
as I shift pain back and forth
at the bus platform.

From the inside,
the windows' night water
glows with colors
no painter could measure.
The leaded glass shapes are apostles
I want to sit beside in a pew.
Outstretched, my cupped hands
could gather the manna
they carry in robe folds.

Where I stand,
wind picks up street litter
and my swollen bones ache.
Yet, it's not enough wind
to fly me over remnants
of forgetting.

If it were night in the city
and priests were saying mass,
the minute streams of light
between downcast lashes
would humble my shoulders
into wings, and I could fly
with hollow bones
into the salt marshes
with a thousand cranes.

California Poppy Chatter

How much can you love me,
ninety-five penciled verses
to my five orange petals,
my narrow short-lived eyes?

Your honor and commitment grow
more leaves than all the trees
to my moody heredity
closing before four o'clock.

But tomorrow, your pencil nibbles
the woody shelf fungus.
Another day, you swallow
the poison nightshade berries.

Your bees pollinate and abandon.
Rambling buzzes burn my cheeks
with phosphorous and shame.

I measure your dreams, promises and praises.
If I were a windflower, could you hold me
as I bend up a steep slope?
Where my roots secure the soil,
can your words endure pelting rain?

Do Bystanders Hear My Hands?

What the chance spectator needs to know
about my converted pickup
I drive with my hands.

Paraplegia is softer than truck gears.
This light, this sound, this joy
come zing on my leftover spine
after months of fluorescent darkness.

I, a hairy lump, tried to vomit the aftershocks,
but nurses invaded my veins
deeper than morphine.
I tried the bathroom, but my legs crumpled.
The crash collapsed all end zones,
pop fly catches, goalie sprints.
Machines detected a myth of legs.
The irascible monitor arm,
the one used to pull me up, broke.
They thought I wouldn't try?

Paraplegia, softer than your truck gears.
Five fingers knob.
The wheel turns.
A hand throttles the gas.
Shoulders grapple with the seat belt,
braking the steep street.
Stop before the dock
of opaque indigo fathoms.
My jeans look intact anyway.

This light, this soft joy,
let's drive on with a leftover spine,
after months of fluorescent darkness.
Play your silver moan, you racing stripes
on my converted blue pick-up.

ELDERBERRY FLUTE

Elderberry Flute

Miwok Madonna meditates
in her gold-threaded scarf,
her wrinkled hands upturned.
She sits straight in her seat,
not leaning into the window
of this commute train.

As in a tule reed boat,
she plies the waters of rivers
come down from grandparents.
A bounty of hands
gathered the land.

My heart paddles upstream to circle
the sacred house and hear
the sacred words, the images
of kin that float on water.

They winnowed this year's seeds.
Let some under the burned duff
be fertilized by ash.
Shoot newborn with spring.

Her grandmother's tawny hands
wove charred redbud into baskets,
to gather the mountain of acorns,
pound the pestle in the grinding rocks,
as other happy fingers
played the elderberry flute.

Without moving her lips,
Madonna chants her tribal tongue
floating onto that shore.

Her grandmother held the childish hands
underwater to feel fish cold,
close to fire to distinguish it from light.
Between their fingers, life
quivered in mother's womb.

Grandma's words couldn't be forgotten:
Don't make your plants cry.
Bend down the branches without breaking
the stems, your kinfolk's legs
when you harvest.
As they grow tall,
their shoots and fruits will teach you
when they are good, show you how to heal.
When elderberry blooms, shellfish are poison.
When berries are sweet,
dig shellfish with relish.
Leave the fallen seeds for the birds,
mice, and next year's harvest.
When goldfinches chatter in the hills,
fill your baskets with blackberries.

That was life before grandmother
was whisked from the watershed.
Before priestly fathers
rounded their bellies with beef.
Before pigs ate acorns.
Before her own mother gathered
sprayed redbuds, numbing her own
mouth, when she touched her lips
in a prayer of thanks
for the special stems.

Sun shines through the gold threads
of her creased hands.
As the train jerks to halt at El Cerrito,
the oracle of hands ceases.
Her lap evaporates into standing legs.
She departs the door
of my heart's pilgrimage.

Madrona Spirit

Open one window
in the ash house wall.
Spinning to the six directions,
the ancestors moan hollow
around the Miwok village.
As words begin to broil,
fog comes rolling over
Olompali Ridge.

Gliding easy as a red tail,
I swing my hips
on the trail up the fault line.

Wind braids tree tops down,
shallowly scooping what is learned.
Madrona mothers planted over
burn patches, watering knowledge
into their children's hands.

But knowing became like hawk feathers,
flipped upside down in wind.
Marin County commissioner
gave five thousand dollars of paper,
for eons of wisdom,
and three thousand acres of earth.
Smoke broke over the rocks.

The unpronounceable names
on sticks in the ground
are shaman healings lost.
When the last Madrona died,
her grinding bowl was broken
and buried.

Olmec Song

Rain floods our fields quiet.
Heat and humidity melt everything.
Drought draws us down into caves.
Chocolate and vanilla thrill a moment only.
Nothing lasts beyond our eyes and fingers.

Forty miles away on the Tuxtla Mountains,
we chisel another carved head.
Axe cracks the rock husk.
He emerges, a new face each time.
He came by boat so many times.
He hears the wind, calls the rain.
In the rock, He does not die.
When His figure is carved, we share
the cup of celebration round.

We make Him ready, together.
We pound fibers into ropes,
woven to hold him, lashed
to the dugout, the new face floats
down the Papaloapan River.

Boys and girls wear woven
clothing to hold them 'til time splits
open their childhood husks.
We share their festival and pass the cup round.

The basalt figure kneels in trance.
Jaguar cloak wrapped.
Planet crowned.
Greenstone eyes, fangs frighten.
Jaw opens, He cries, a hungry baby.

His third eye is a diamond
round a birth circle.
God lives in this rock.
He hears the wind,
calls the rain to Tres Zapotes,
where we dance His dance.
He sees our milpa
of maize, beans and squash—
two years toil, eight fallow.
He orders—
three sisters flip out seeds.

Jerusalem Artichoke Flowers

Daisy-like heads lift
laughing above my head.
On hunger's wind,
goldfinches undulate in for seeds.
Claws cling to strong stems
that bend to earth
with fifteen foot springs.
The laugh carries from flower to belly.
How easily they grew
from the tubers we planted.
I didn't know they would grow so high,
bloom so freely
laugh so completely,
or feed so many birds.

Premature Spring

"After one day, maybe next week
after ice storms wrapping trees. . ."
        —Diane Frank, from "Floating Redwoods in the Early Morning"

A pulse comes, barely warm
pushing to release.

In the lee between snow drifts,
a green tuft turns its head.
Water to bathe the sprouted bulb
freezes into glass.
The sprout u-turns
back under winter.

Driven into the clearing,
birthlings await her full udders.
Marshmallow deer
scoops snow with her paw,
nibbles and arches her head.
Sharp stomps from her, seeing me
because prey do that, alerting.
Her shirring strides diminish
as if she never left the
leafless tree shadows.

Hooves can hardly
breech the ice.
Let the song of blood
refrain until pillowed snow melts,
the swollen streams flow,
and her fawns reach
to chew above the leaf line,
before the hunt begins.

Wild Plum Orchestra

The orchestra holds its breath
for the plum leaf baton.

One feather makes a motion
upwind from shrubs.
Cave tubes are opening.

The hollow chamber
where triangles have their start
pulls shoulders back
to sustain a flow.
The whole body opens
to a higher elevation.

The refuge remembers
they own their own keys.
They haven't yet begun to play
but arch their bows to listen.

GATHERING WILDNESS

The Talon Test

I could choose the backsides
of two other churches,
while kneeling in the bird blind.
Across the road, ordained concrete
heaves its shields of stone.
Where eyes fitted to pews and nave don't go,
one rectory door uncages
through rain puddles, scalding sun,
and wing-breaking wind.
The other screens its whip-poor-will parson
from beak clicks by a jail of lattice.
In this region of repose, detachment
is a dust bath for feathers.

With old sore knees I ladder
shoulders up to the willow window.
Through glass I choose my flight
where a footpath twists into quicksand.
Tiny brown, under brush, coming to teeter
on the buttress of cattails,
the marsh wren flits and brags,
never consulting a hymnal.

My sweaty palms turn the glass
to check for enemies in trees.
A bulwark of faces and voices
can't shield us as we glide
from prey above the swamp,
naked to the talon test.

Mirage of Shore Birds

When the arches of your feet
ache to surrender
to the sirens of the shore,
you take the long gravel walk
through greasy winter sunshine
over lifetimes of Mare Island sediment.
Even after a mile trek,
the huddle clucks further out.
Unsteady hands bounce the binoculars,
twisting the focal point,
while they waddle, skitter and mate.
The moment glass connects image to name,
that duck dives under.
Gathering wildness is not mirage.

Farther away at Skaggs Island,
the birds come shrill, wailing in your sleep,
urging your belly to make muscle candy
to the haven of burrowing owls.
You identify the kestrel's ki ki ki
as your own blood, trying to fly.

When the arcade of work
sucks your heels backward,
and the tide fills in your sand tracks
with the backwash of money,
you run, a corpuscle, to commuter trains.
Overhead, the ki ki ki repeats.
That endangered weekend
could have been another life.

Flamenco Scientist

In wilds of my backyard,
a sharp-eyed girl
spikes a mist of tiny flies
with raptorial forelegs.
She hides in plain sight.

She is hooked to the spur
of a never ending hunger,
steel eyes, castanet clippers.
Ambush in the camouflage of light.

She's going to embrace the chest
of her prey, biting off their heads.
Hiding from scorpions,
preying mantis is masked in grass.

Stuck on the sidewall of a tire,
I rescue this stick with switchblade legs.
Unfolding the dish cloth,
I lay her pregnant in castaway brush.
Matchsticks erupt in spring.
Ambush in the camouflage of light.

Pruning the Plum Wall

The plum trees come to rule.
A canopy, the second story
darkens a dungeon over the avocado
and backyard kingdoms of life.
My jumping jacks attack
the wide torso trunks.
I squeeze long handled clippers,
amputate the incarcerating branches
and shake down bunches
to the ivory groundcover.
Prune 'til the hinges open
to the republic of wings.

From the sun god of auguring light
the capacitor thrills
and light charges the ground.

My fighting thumbs give up
when the pile of limbs
reaches to my shoulders.

I trounced the plum of its green greed.
The understory bursts with wild light.
Everything that flies leaves
a draft of painted wings

Eagle Banding

Wing feathers trapped
to heal a broken wing,
her freedom is gripped
in fingers of a big man's chest.
Biologists who healed her
kneel in awe.

At Las Trampas, a net bands
above her skin tearing claws,
to chart her sky wheel
when she's released.

Her eyes dilate
kingship over the canopy,
scouring for mates
ferocious for rivals.

Her cawing cracks
open hope, grows our wings
as she escapes upward,
so like the last shrill
of small lives sacrificed
for her wild flesh.

RED SHOULDERED MENTOR

For Diane Frank

For beaks, in place of tongues.

Each feather of her red shoulders broadens the air.
Bird bodhisattva drops talons
carefully around our clutch.
We nest in a cypress on the edge of the continent.
White caps roll incessantly.

Life's imperative—eat the yoke of this weekend.
My egg tooth knocks.
Crack the parchment imagery
of every poem where I died,
where vermin dissected my metaphors.

Her beak tears the bones of furry creatures
who would steal our succulent rawness.
Her tones shout above wave crash.
We gorge on each tidbit.
Muscles fatten, feathers lengthen.

Preparing to fledge, we don't study dart guns.
Trying wings, we break nesting sticks.
How largely our long wings displace the air!
Seer, she knows our first flight
will drop us through jagged needles.

Her Monday beak nudges our tails.
Fear flies over the western sea.
We scatter as wheel spokes
sharpening our beaks.
I imagine dive bombing the doubters.
Revolving a wing rearward,
I caw a salute to my red shouldered mentor.

Against the Twinkle of Star Time

Against the twinkle of star time,
my ear drum ticks, my heart's tiny hum.
Against the pillared nebula of creation,
human clocks stop.
Our black and white vacillates
under eon arcs of star lives.

The nightstand watch sweeps
its arms around the pillowed night
to trap diligence in its wrist buckle.
Against the drone of eagle-eyed teachers,
students are tethered to school desks.
Fingers chafe irregular beats
against the incentive to write.
Their pricked hearts seek spring sun
veining leaves outside the corbelled arch,
the city roar and mammalian history.

Sun appears to fade in the west
against half-sized humans yammering for food.
Appliance timers mark the finished rice and beans.
Battery metronomes flick the score
against the explosion of newborn stars.
Something whispers,
and the heart beats in the throat,
to push the mind straight through the night,
to break free of time.

WIDE BODIED PELICANS

Rancho Seco in April

Start from the nuclear cooling tower
southeast of Sacramento, with narrow waist,
colossal height, and neutered core.
It is one of many mausoleums.

The Temple to Artemis,
one of seven ancient wonders,
merges into debris.
Her statue, a many breasted fountain,
streaming water from every nipple,
is rubble in Ephesus.

Newton's apple replaced
the craving for the clout of Greek gods.
The brainchild of Einstein
launched mushroom pollination—
human annihilation.

We drive past ghosts of old paradigms
that run like jet streams,
from this unburied dead tower,
toward the reservoir,
smoldering with spring.

Our feet tread a fisherman's track.
We begin reeling in promise
that doesn't remember radiation:
miner's lettuce, owl-faced clover,
bedstraw, and small patches of poison oak.
We stretch and explore the rim,
which by nature opens
to the surge of our watery planet.

Wide-bodied pelicans,
sturdy as aluminum jet planes
glide over the sun-gem azure water.
Into cottonwood flirting trees
violet-green swallows flock.
The finger-sized females swag
and mate with their storefronts.

Under black walnut and buckeye catkins,
we keep climbing uphill.
Sun rises in cattle pastures
in the yellow chest of the meadowlark.
His claws sharpen rusty barbed wire.
He voices pure sounds,
the crystal chandelier our ears forgot.

Over the backside of the lake,
eager teenagers of woodpeckers
tap amassed pressure.
Marsh wrens we don't see
chat unceasingly,
girls at a slumber party.

We rest arthritic elbows
piled on a picnic table of experience.
The best efforts splintering atoms
or building towers up to the Goddess
come from heavy boned humans.
When Her spirits fly,
Her splendor reaches the trees.
She bestows spring in the sun of April.

Sluggish Sunset

This could be the last night
my eyes are good enough
to power my BMW bubble
up the double orange street stripe,
careening around fearful drivers
to Shadi's Bethlehem in El Cerrito.

Paying bills with paper checks,
my fingers trace longhand
the hard press of numerals.
At my wooden first grade desk,
tears erased the pencil's effort.
Lefty third grade cursive,
built a middle finger callous
against the right-handed school.
Blue signature scrawling
into engraved walls of granite,
within dried ink wells.

With farsighted children in my lap,
unwrap their wonder book
to plates of birds: bug catching
bushtits and dagger beaked pelicans,
scarlet wings and swallow tails.
In the cell phone match song to photo.
Soon enough, their calls
will color only memory.

Sunset going down slowly,
preparing for the all-at-once
drop into the starless sea.
Urgently, fingertips build nerves,
an awl drilling into heartwood.

Drive to take the Braille touch,
but how--topography of California
under the hood of a book?

I weed the curving edge of each flower bed,
tenderly editing thread knots of word weeds.
Imagine an embroidered hoop of damask,
magenta, muslin and coral azaleas,
grown over tended years.
I name each verse in honor of a loved one:
Clinton, May, Ruth, whose eyes fly
untouched by barricades of earth.

With opened eyes I scan the yard.
Ivory calla lily, pumpkin nasturtium,
buxom hydrangea, fragrant kaffir lime,
foretell the shadow
that leaves only aroma,
the spectacle of Christmas green.

Blinking won't tear away the glaucous haze.
Put away the flashlights, candles, spotlights.
No need for paper sheets or handheld phones.
Bicycles, BMW, put them away, too.

No need for ears.
Throw them in the trash.
If you can't have eyes,
let fragrance be the last sense
lingering, a coffin bouquet.
Let the lost remnants
be a barnyard of rotten onion.

Tipping Rhythm

for Robert Creeley

It's all a rhythm
from train surge
to freeway wedge.
Eyelashes open
the commute doors open
their moons, their waterfalls
good will and money flowing.

The roll of the day
rising from bowed knees
pleasing whatsoever is needed.
Familiar as self, recurring
frustration and delay, chest rising.
Rising the vague relays
of all the selves watching
waterfalls jump, the mist melting
into love, eyes shining,
father holding daughter frightened,
mother tugging son,
runs up the stairs.
Heart holds breath.
Is this it, really it?

Structure of industry and trees
sunspot stop lights.
The current dominant white man
guiding legs at crosswalks,
eyes to cubicles.
Take me whole hollow fullness
joy of the heart song.
Scratch through headache
of details, retail blue
to rusted junkyards of afternoon.

Her variegated sweater croons
the headache and heartache
taken hostage, bowing
in servitude
to hollow fullness.

Taking a bullet,
dodging a knife,
talking them out of revenge
or stealing trucks for spite.
Give them the gold
growing good will
of full waterfalls, if
they can rise up and drink.

Dancing the rhythms
hip deep in thrill.
Isness with the god love
man in your body.
Hips otherwise scream
with childbirth in their bones.

Dragging the watering hose
to wash children,
all the clothes of earth.
Dull lumbar ache
rising from four-legged humility.
Hoarding cups
tools, machines, mortar.
Copper opportunities
to rise above others,
prosper amid their misery.

But women's rhythms weave
linen, wool, reeds
red-waisted marriage cloths,
hoping for time outside the hive.

Where does it go,
with sun, moon and pole star
the last faces one sees
burning eyes goodbye?
I, wanting to be free.
I am, separating
from eye socket earth.
That unknown lifts
us all to defy gravity.
What each I questions,
finds a way to answers in galaxies
no lips can shape, nor glories fathom;
and may find blossoms in a garland of stars.

The Gate of Guilt

Sunset catches fire in car mirrors.
Their hands froze on steering wheels.
Stars vacillate over trapped drivers.
City warehouses are a vacuum of sky.
A mile of headlights, arteries and veins,
traffic stops for the dead.
How heavy are their hearts?

Bacteria pierce radiators and pores of skin.
Not arriving at judgment,
they single out the divided highway.
They invade despite the force of fear and anger.
They begin to eat the humans' weight.

Let them lighten each heart on the scale
of the *Egyptian Book of the Dead*.
To board the star of tomorrow,
balance on the scale of tonight,
light as the ostrich feather of Ma'at.

Parade after Hurricane Sandy

I stare from the home flat screen
into the chilled New York street.
The crowd's breathe forges
like their hands, yoked
to hold the helium balloons.
Thanksgiving survives.

Gritty stories chatter
about storm surges, shattering rain,
the dice roll of devastation.

They gather momentum
over maple street trees.
Rising with the strings,
they rebound from gilded edges
of burnished beryl windows.

Black and white placards
shout each borough's voice.
Their shoulders hook a serried line.
They roll a torch up Fifth Avenue.
Horns brag to the world's cameras.
The future skims over
this hurricane eclipse
of their legendary sky.

About the Author

Melissa Hobbs supervised a team who dedicated themselves to help injured workers heal and re-enter the work world. After a career with State Compensation Insurance Fund, she returns to poetry, where she once began her writing career at Kent State University in Ohio. She is published across the U.S. Her first book brings forth pomegranates of hope, streams that flow under bankrupt cities and in fasting deserts, and wings to climb above the talons of predators.

www.ingramcontent.com/pod-product-compliance
Lightning Source LLC
Chambersburg PA
CBHW032017090426
42741CB00006B/633